I
AM
RESPONSIBLE

WONDERFULLY ANOINTED! Following these principles of God, you can only look forward to a truly blessed relationship.

—*Clara Puckett*

This handbook is a good quick reference for the man on the go!

—*Howard Miller*

As a Sunday school teacher and counselor for young married couples, the one thing I recognize is that most of the young men do not know what a Godly husband should be. This anointed book cuts through all the fluff and tells it like God meant it to be. It should be required reading for premarital counseling.

—*JoAnn Auger*

STAR! Read it now, cover to cover; its pages are an anointed adventure worthy of travel.

—*Mizell Campbell*

I
AM
RESPONSIBLE

Jennie Staten

YAV PUBLICATIONS
ASHEVILLE, NORTH CAROLINA

Copyright © 2015 by Jennie Staten

Scriptures quoted are from the *The Holy Bible*, King James Version. New York: American Bible Society: 1999.

Second Edition

ISBN: 978-1-937449-05-6

Published by:

YAV PUBLICATIONS
ASHEVILLE, NORTH CAROLINA

YAV books may be purchased in bulk for educational, business, fund-raising, or sales promotional use. For information, contact Books@yav.com or phone toll-free 888-693-9365.

Visit our website: www.InterestingWriting.com

3 5 7 9 10 8 6 4 2

Published August 2015

Printed and Assembled in the United States of America

DEDICATION

I would like to dedicate the writing of this book to my mother, Mrs. Bertha Staten, who has demonstrated the strength of a strong woman; her philosophy is "always tell the truth, be honest, and love God."

To my father, Hosea Staten (deceased) who always believed in me and encouraged me that God had a special plan for my life.

To my baby sister, Maria Denise Staten (deceased) who looked up to her big sister and always showed me much love and respect.

I thank the Lord for parents who laid a foundation for me to build a relationship with my Lord and Savior Jesus Christ.

Thank you!

Jennie Staten

ACKNOWLEDGEMENTS

I want to thank all the women from our Tuesday Morning Bible Study for their support. A special "Thank you" to Mr. & Mrs. Garland Puckett, Mr. & Mrs. Howard Miller, Mr. & Mrs. Mizell Campbell, Mrs. Janice Ivey, Mrs. JoAnn Auger, Mrs. Doris Turner, Mrs. Pamela Panzico, and Dr. Myles Munroe (deceased, November 9, 2014), Bahamas Faith Ministries for their encouragement. My deepest gratitude to Ms. Juanita Jones, Ms. Gaye Putman, and Mr. Ronald Phillips for their help in preparing this manuscript for publication.

In Honor of Dr. Myles Munroe

Dr. Myles Munroe, Spiritual Papa, who encouraged me to "die empty," never taking my dreams and purpose to the grave.

CONTENTS

INTRODUCTION

The purpose of this handbook is to help men understand their role in the home, both spiritually and physically.

Man's first duty and obligation is to God. Secondly, it is to his wife; not his children, job, mom, dad, sister, brother, friend, etc.! You see, the relationship between the husband and wife will be the greatest influence on the children. The home is the training ground and Mom and Dad have the control. You can train your children to be honest or dishonest, loving, or hateful by what you demonstrate to them in the home.

PROVERBS 20: 6–7 *"Most men will proclaim every one his own goodness: but a faithful man who can find?* [7] *The just man walketh in his integrity; his children are blessed after him."*

This scripture confirms why husband and wife must be in harmony with each other, in order to properly mold and shape their children. Children do what they see more than what they are told.

A powerful quote spoken by Coach Wooten, former Coach of UCLA, states, "No printed word or oral plan or all the books on all the shelves can teach our youth what they should be. It's what the teachers are themselves."

Men, God has given you the authority. This book will help you understand the power of agreement between you and your wife so that you can be Godly parents and a role model of God's design for the family.

I pray that your heart and mind be open and that you allow the Holy Spirit to minister God's truth to you. When the husband and wife's relationship is in obedience to God's Word, everyone benefits — your family, church, city, state, and the world.

I

IN THE BEGINNING

In the beginning, Satan had a plan to destroy what God had blessed and joined: man and wife, in the institution of marriage. In the garden, he purposed to devalue woman in man's sight, and cause him to question and doubt God's love for him. This plan was set in motion when the serpent came to Eve.

Satan attacks first in the area where he can have the biggest impact: the authority figure, the leader, the man in charge. Yes, he went to Eve for she was the vehicle he would use to influence Adam to disobey God's word and then blame God and Eve for his decision.

What was Eve's motive? Why did she listen to the serpent? What was she thinking? Eve knew the serpent was God's creation and what he said to her sounded good and made sense. It soon became obvious that she was not sure about the commandment concerning the forbidden fruit. She told the serpent she could not eat from the tree in the midst of the garden. God had given Adam the commandment not to eat from the tree of The Knowledge of Good and Evil before Eve came on the scene. Evidently, Adam did not make this clear to Eve.

The Bible clearly states that Eve was deceived, and no one can deceive you about something that you really know in your heart to be true. It is when you are not sure that you can be deceived. That is why the Lord commands us to read His Word and hide it in our hearts that we may not sin against Him and we may be able to discern the truth.

Satan uses the lack of knowledge of God's Word to bring destruction. I believe Eve felt the information she was receiving from the serpent could help her husband. She thought she was operating in her purpose, which was to be a helpmate for Adam. God is perfect! When God creates or makes something, it functions the way God designs it to until it becomes defiled. Eve had no knowledge of evil at this point, so there is no way she might have been trying to undermine her husband's authority. Eve did not just react; she pondered what the serpent told her. *She looked and saw that the tree was good for food, and that it was pleasant to the eyes, and to be desired to make one wise, she took the fruit thereof, and did eat, and gave also unto her husband with her; and he did eat.* Eve's intentions were to help and honor her husband. If she really believed that by eating the fruit they would die, then she protected her husband by eating it first.

Either way you look at it, you would have to know that she was trying to help her husband. It would be like saying to God, which Adam did, that everything was fine before you gave me this woman. You gave her to me not to help me, but to function as a means to rip my inheritance from me. No! Eve was God's gift to Adam and God always gives good gifts (JAMES 1:17).

When Eve ate first and nothing physically happened, her eyes were not opened and neither were her husband's...she assumed it was safe to give the fruit to him. Adam was to protect his wife and make sure she understood God's instructions to them. Adam made a conscious decision to eat the fruit instead of obeying the commandment of the Lord. God would not have allowed Eve to eat without her husband being present, because God had given authority over the garden to Adam. God made them one, Adam would have been separated from Eve and alone again if only she had eaten the fruit and died spiritually. It might have seemed like God had made a mistake in giving Eve to Adam because it would not last. Many times we as Christians do the same thing; we go by what we see instead of obeying God's word. That's not faith.

In 1 TIMOTHY 2:14, it states that Eve was deceived, which means to be tricked or mislead. God cursed the world for Adam's disobedience and not for Eve having been deceived. DEUTERONOMY 11:26–28 & CHAPTER 28. When God came looking for them in the garden, whose name did he call? Adam's! Yes, God punished Eve for the part she played in the fall of humanity, because there is always a consequence for doing wrong, whether purposely or not. The consequence is a reminder to keep you from making the same mistake again. However, notice God in His goodness and mercy did not take away the joy of motherhood, but added pain as a reminder. Adam was working to cultivate and take care of the garden before he disobeyed, but sweat and labor was added as a reminder of his disobedience.

So how did Satan plan to devalue woman? By causing her husband to disrespect her advice or opinion. Consider what happened when Adam listened to his wife — he lost everything. Satan also planned for man not to fully trust God. Adam had everything, and suddenly, God brings woman on the scene and she causes him to lose it all. In the back of Adam's mind, he blamed God, thus hindering his faith in Him.

Today many men still blame their wife for many of their problems and are reluctant to receive the good counsel that can come from them. Jesus took the shame and the blame so that leaves no place to continue blaming each other. Rather, put your trust in God because He always has our best interest at heart.

I say to you, if you have a wife who loves the Lord, and she is a student of the Word, and faithful in prayer; there is no other person, except for the Holy Spirit, who can give you better council than her. She is your covenant partner, your helper, and your gift from God!

2

I AM RESPONSIBLE

What does it mean to be *responsible?*
"Obliged or expected to account for or to do, deserving credit or blame; trustworthy, able to tell right from wrong."

Men, I know this may surprise you, but—you are RESPONSIBLE for your wife and children. God has given you this responsibility as the authority figure in your home. I CORINTHIANS 11:3

Why did the Lord say, *"Therefore shall a man leave his father and his mother, and shall cleave unto his wife, and they two shall be one flesh"* GENESIS 2:24. When you are home with your father and mother, you are the child under the authority of your parents. When you marry, both your position and role changes and God has a new set of responsibilities for you as head of your household.

"...and shall cleave unto his wife and they two shall be one flesh." Cleave means to hold fast or cling to. Most men cannot comprehend their wives as a part of them in this physical world because they came into the relationship as two individuals; however, it is spiritually that the two become one.

As parents, we are sometimes more committed to our children than to our spouse because we can comprehend how in the physical world it required something from both the husband (sperm) and the wife (egg) to produce a child and because of that, we know that they are a part of us. In the same manner, husband and wife must feel that total commitment to each other because when they marry, they are one spiritually.

Most men feel responsible for their family's physical needs, but what about their Spiritual needs? Because God is a Spirit, should not men focus their attention on the Spiritual needs of the family and let God take care of the physical. John 4:24, Matthew 6:31–34.

God has his order.

I Corinthians 11:3 states, *"But I would have you know, that the head of every man is Christ and the head of the woman is the man; and the head of Christ is God."*

When husband and wife are out of God's order, meaning the woman is leading spiritually instead of the man, it is like a train with the cars before the engine. They cannot move as they should because the engine is pushing against the cars instead of leading them.

No matter how successful the woman is, she has not reached her potential if the husband is not leading the family spiritually.

3

SUBMISSION

PHESIANS 5:22 says *"Wives, submit yourselves unto your own husband, as unto the Lord."*

Of course, this is a favorite scripture of many men and I think it is because they have totally misunderstood it and taken it completely out of context. Submit means *to respond or to come up under and follow* and wives were designed to respond automatically and follow their husbands.

If someone smiles at you, the automatic response is to smile back. If someone waves at you, the automatic response is to wave back. If someone yawns, the automatic response is to yawn.

You do not have to think about these things; it is just an automatic reflex. The same applies to the husband and wife when they are following God's plan; if you are kind to her, she will be kind to you; if you love her, she will automatically love you and so on.

Many women, when they are mistreated, try to pretend that everything is okay and overlook that they have an abusive husband. Such abuse can be physical, emotional, or verbal. They hide their hurt and pain and pretend that nothing is wrong. This unnatural response does not signal to the husband that he has done something wrong and bitterness and resentment can come into the wife's heart against him.

EPHESIANS 4:26, 31 says *"Let all bitterness, wrath, anger, clamor, and evil speaking be put away from you, with all malice. Be ye angry, and sin not: let not the sun go down upon your wrath."*

This can only be accomplished if you express your true feelings in love.

You have seen women that were soft-spoken, meek, mild, and sweet; but after being married to an abusive husband, they turned into FRANKEN*(STEEN).* This transformation is caused by bottled up anger that has become explosive because it was not expressed and handled in love.

Men, be that safe place that your wife can come to knowing that regardless to what's going on in her emotions, she will be OK once she can get to you.

4

WIVES NEVER GRADUATE FROM THEIR HUSBAND'S RESPONSIBILITY AND AUTHORITY!

As far as God is concerned, husbands are like parents/guardian to their wives. If your child is at school fighting and being disobedient, who is the school going to call? The parent or guardian.

If your child broke a neighbor's window, the first thing a responsible parent would say is, "I will pay for it or have my insurance take care of it." Why? Because they know that they are responsible for their child's actions.

Why did Joshua say: "As for me and my house, we will serve the Lord"? JOSHUA 24:15

Why did Sarah call Abraham, "Lord"?

Eve ate the fruit first, but it did not become sin until Adam ate. Whom did God hold accountable? ROMANS 5:12–14. Just as Adam was responsible for Eve's actions, so is the husband responsible for his wife's.

Jesus was responsible for His disciples because God had given them to His charge. John 17:8–26

This isn't to imply that the wife does not have to answer for herself; she is responsible for her own actions, but so are you. Men, God has placed the power within you to help develop your wife into what she needs to be so that she can be used for His service. Daniel 12:13 Psalm 16:5. You need to realize this, because one day you will stand before the Creator and give an account for both yourself and your family.

5

WIVES ARE MIRRORS OF THEIR HUSBANDS

What you see in your wife is like looking into a mirror.

It is a reflection of what you have given to her. It is a resemblance of your relationship with the heavenly Father. EPHESIANS 5:28 says *"So ought men to love their wives as their own bodies. He that loveth his wife loveth himself."* Why? Because more than likely, what you see in her is what you have given. I challenge you men to name all the things you do not particularly like about your wife, and it will show you the things you need to work on to make your marriage better.

> **Example:**   You might say, "She does not consider my needs."
> **Reflection:** Do you consider her needs?
> **Example:**   She does not listen.
> **Reflection:** Do you listen to her?

In EPHESIANS 5:25, Paul compares the relationship of a husband and wife to that of Christ and the Church.

Therefore, Ephesians 5:25–27 can be read like this: "Husbands, love your wives, even as Christ loved the church, and gave himself for it; that the husband might sanctify and cleanse his wife with the washing of the Word. That the husband might present his wife to himself a glorious wife, not having spot, or wrinkle, or any such thing; but that she should be whole and without blemish." IMPOSSIBLE! No… God would never ask you to do something if it wasn't possible for you to do. The Blood of Jesus is what cleansed the Church and restored our broken fellowship back to God. Husbands, the Word of God is what cleanses your wife to help keep her in fellowship with God. You should help keep her clean to be used by God, just as the Blood of Jesus cleanses us when we make a mistake and repent.

How do I cleanse my wife with the Word?

- By first planting the Word of God in your heart and teaching it diligently to your family.
- By having family devotions and handling life's situations according to the principles outlined in God's Word.
- Let her see the Word operating in your life.

A Godly wife can help change her husband's life. The scripture says "and the woman who hath a husband that believeth not, and if he be pleased to dwell with her, let her not leave him. For the unbelieving husband is sanctified by the wife, and the unbelieving wife is sanctified by the husband." I Corinthians 7:13, 14

The Lord is showing you the power of His Spirit "because greater is He that is in you than he that is in the world."

Now if the woman, being the weaker vessel, can sanctify an unbelieving husband; think of what a positive influence you can be upon your wife given your position of authority.

Men, if you would love your wives the way Christ loved the Church, your wife would not dwell on your faults because that Love you give will cover a multitude of sins. Love "is not puffed up, doth not behave itself unseemly, seeketh not her own, is not easily provoked, thinketh no evil; rejoiceth not in iniquity, but rejoiceth in the truth; beareth all things, believeth all things, hopeth all things, endureth all things. LOVE never faileth!" I Corinthians 13:4–8

You don't have to worry about a vicious or contentious woman when you allow the love of Jesus Christ to flow through you. That is what she will see; that is what she will respond to.

6

WHATSOEVER A MAN SOWETH, THAT SHALL HE ALSO REAP...

S ow means to *plant*. Reap means to *receive the fruit of your planting*.

If you plant good seeds in your wife and cultivate and nourish those seeds, you will produce an increase in your relationship.

"Be not deceived; God is not mocked: for whatsoever a man soweth, that shall he also reap. For he that soweth to his flesh shall of the flesh reap corruption; but he that soweth to the Spirit shall of the Spirit reap life everlasting," Galatians 6:7, 8.

"But this I say, he which soweth sparingly shall reap also sparingly; and he which soweth bountifully shall reap also bountifully." II Corinthians 9:6

"Give, and it shall be given unto you; good measure, pressed down, shaken together, and running over, shall men give into your bosom. For with the same measure that ye mete withal it shall be measured to you again." Luke 6:38

"The kingdom of heaven is like to a grain of mustard seed, which a man took, and sowed in his field: Which indeed is the least of all seeds: but when it is grown, it is the greatest

among herbs, and becometh a tree, so that the birds of the air come and lodge in the branches thereof." MATTHEW 13:31–32

"But he that received seed into the good ground is he that heareth the word, and understandeth it; which also beareth fruit, and brought forth, some a hundredfold, some sixty, some thirty." MATTHEW 13:23

7

WHAT ARE GOOD SEEDS?

1. *Love*. Telling your wife you love her without showing it will cause her to doubt your love. I John 3:18–19

2. *Importance*. She must feel that she is the most important person in your life next to God.

3. *Partnership*. She must feel like she is a part of your life; do not make important decisions without talking it over with her first.

4. *Direction*. Always point your family to Jesus. Teach them to turn to God in times of trouble and need.

5. *Sensitivity*. Be sensitive to your wife's need. Make her feel safe to come to you with anything she is feeling, even if it does not make sense to you; be compassionate and caring.

6. *Listening*. Be a good listener. Very often the Lord speaks through your wife.

7. *Affection*. Be kind and gentle always. Love her and touch her even when you do not want to engage in sexual intimacy. Say kind words to her and compliment her.

8. *Be a Father*. If you have children, be a good father to them. By being a good Father, you teach

your children how to love and trust their heavenly Father. It does the wife's heart good to see you love your children.

9. *Self denial*. There will be times when you will need to put your wife's needs before your own and times she will put your needs before hers.

10. *Forgiveness*. You must be willing to forgive and be forgiven. Unforgiveness opens the door to bitterness, anger, and resentment.

If you plant cotton, you get cotton; if you plant beans you get beans. The same principle applies; if you plant love, kindness, gentleness, etc., that is what you will get back. II Corinthians 9:6, Galatians 6:7–9

Men, your family members will never be all that God has called them to be if you yourself do not have a personal relationship with God. You must spend time in prayer and in the Word daily. You might have many complaints about your wife, but tell me: Does she see you spending time in the Word? Does she see you spending time in prayer? Does she see you praise and worship the Lord freely? Does she see the love of God lived out in you? As scripture informs us, what you are speaking out of your mouth reveals what is in your heart. Matthew 12:33–37

Maybe you need to take a look inside yourself first. If God tells you three times in Ephesians chapter 5, to love your wife, then when you do that, something happens spiritually against which all the demons in hell cannot prevail.

8

THE POWER PRAYER

I believe the prayers of agreement between a husband and wife are the most effective prayers that you can pray. I PETER 3:7–12, MATTHEW 18:19. I believe the devil is also aware of this power and that is why he works so hard to bring division between the husband and wife. He is doing a heck of a job keeping husband and wife divided, wouldn't you say?

The way you treat your wife is like an investment. If you invest wisely, you get a good return. PROVERBS 18:22 says "Whoso findeth a wife findeth a good thing and obtaineth favor with the Lord." Which means, God will favor your investment and give you a good return.

REMEMBER: A wife is in the hand of the husband as the clay is in the potter's hand. The husband can mold and shape the wife into a beautiful piece of art or a bruised and broken vessel.

THE CHOICE IS YOURS!

Pray this prayer:

Heavenly Father, in the Name of Jesus, I confess that I have not been the Spiritual covering I should have been for my family. I ask you to forgive me and help me to be the husband you have called me to be. I know that unless the Lord builds the house, we labor in vain and that a house divided against itself shall fall. I pray that my relationship with my wife and family will be one of unity because where there is unity there is power and strength. Thank you for your forgiveness, love, wisdom, guidance, and direction. I commit my ways to you and ask you to be the Lord of everything I say and do. In Jesus' Name, I pray Amen.

REFERENCE STUDY

King James Version

INTRODUCTION

PROVERBS 20:6–7

"Most men will proclaim every one his own goodness: but a faithful man who can find? ⁷The just man walketh in his integrity: his children are blessed after him."

CHAPTER ONE

1 CORINTHIANS 11:3

"But I would have you know, that the head of every man is Christ; and the head of the woman is the man; and the head of Christ is God."

GENESIS 2:24

"Therefore shall a man leave his father and his mother, and shall cleave unto his wife: and they shall be one flesh."

JOHN 4:24

"God is a Spirit: and they that worship him must worship him in spirit and in truth."

MATTHEW 6:31–34

"Therefore take no thought, saying, What shall we eat? or What shall we drink? or Wherewithal shall we be clothed?

[32] *(For after all these things do the Gentiles seek:) for your heavenly Father knoweth that ye have need of all these things.* [33] *But seek ye first the kingdom of God, and his righteousness; and all these things shall be added unto you.* [34] *Take therefore no thought for the morrow: for the morrow shall take thought for the things of itself. Sufficient unto the day is the evil thereof."*

Chapter Two

Ephesians 5:22

"Wives, submit yourselves unto your own husbands, as unto the Lord."

Ephesians 4:26

"Be ye angry, and sin not: let not the sun go down upon your wrath. [31] *Let all bitterness, and wrath, and anger, and clamour, and evil speaking, be put away from you, with all malice…"*

Chapter Three

Joshua 24:15

"And if it seem evil unto you to serve the Lord, choose you this day whom ye will serve; whether the gods which your fathers served that were on the other side of the flood, or the gods of the Amorites, in whose land ye dwell: but as for me and my house, we will serve the Lord."

Romans 5:12–14

"Wherefore, as by one man sin entered into the world, and death by sin; and so death passed upon all men, for that all have sinned: [13] *(for until the law sin was in the world: but sin is not imputed when there is no law.* [14] *Nevertheless death*

reigned *from Adam to Moses, even over them that had not sinned after the similitude of Adam's transgression, who is the figure of him that was to come."*

John 17:8–26

"For I have given unto them the words which thou gavest me; and they have received them, and have known surely that I came out from thee, and they have believed that thou didst send me. [9]I pray for them: I pray not for the world, but for them which thou hast given me; for they are thine. [10]And all mine are thine, and thine are mine; and I am glorified in them.

[11]And now I am no more in the world, but these are in the world, and I come to thee. Holy Father, keep through thine own name those whom thou hast given me, that they may be one, as we are. [12]While I was with them in the world, I kept them in thy name: those that thou gavest me I have kept, and none of them is lost, but the son of perdition; that the scripture might be fulfilled.

[13]And now come I to thee; and these things I speak in the world, that they might have my joy fulfilled in themselves. [14]I have given them thy word; and the world hath hated them, because they are not of the world, even as I am not of the world. [15]I pray not that thou shouldest take them out of the world, but that thou shouldest keep them from the evil. [16]They are not of the world, even as I am not of the world. [17]Sanctify them through thy truth: thy word is truth. [18]As thou hast sent me into the world, even so have I also sent them into the world. [19]And for their sakes I sanctify myself, that they also might be sanctified through the truth.

[20]Neither pray I for these alone, but for them also which shall believe on me through their word; [21]that they all may be one; as thou, Father, art in me, and I in thee, that they also

may be one in us: that the world may believe that thou hast sent me. ²²*And the glory which thou gavest me I have given them; that they may be one, even as we are one:* ²³*I in them, and thou in me, that they may be made perfect in one; and that the world may know that thou hast sent me, and hast loved them, as thou hast loved me.*

²⁴*Father, I will that they also, whom thou hast given me, be with me where I am; that they may behold my glory, which thou hast given me: for thou lovedst me before the foundation of the world.* ²⁵*O righteous Father, the world hath not known thee: but I have known thee, and these have known that thou hast sent me.* ²⁶*And I have declared unto them thy name, and will declare it: that the love wherewith thou hast loved me may be in them, and I in them."*

Daniel 12:13

"But go thou thy way till the end be: for thou shalt rest, and stand in thy lot at the end of the days."

Psalm 16:5

"The Lord is the portion of mine inheritance and of my cup: thou maintainest my lot."

Chapter Four

Ephesians 5:28

"So ought men to love their wives as their own bodies. He that loveth his wife loveth himself."

Ephesians 5:25–27

"Husbands, love your wives, even as Christ also loved the church, and gave himself for it; ²⁶*that he might sanctify and cleanse it with the washing of water by the word,* ²⁷*that he*

might present it to himself a glorious church, not having spot, or wrinkle, or any such thing; but that it should be holy and without blemish."

1 Corinthians 7:13–14

"And the woman which hath an husband that believeth not, and if he be pleased to dwell with her, let her not leave him. [14]For the unbelieving husband is sanctified by the wife, and the unbelieving wife is sanctified by the husband: else were your children unclean; but now are they holy."

1 Corinthians 13:4–8

"Love suffereth long, and is kind; Love envieth not; Love vaunteth not itself, is not puffed up, [5]doth not behave itself unseemly, seeketh not her own, is not easily provoked, thinketh no evil; [6]rejoiceth not in iniquity, but rejoiceth in the truth; [7]Beareth all things, believeth all things, hopeth all things, endureth all things. [8]Love never faileth: but whether there be prophecies, they shall fail; whether there be tongues, they shall cease; whether there be knowledge, it shall vanish away."

Chapter Five

Galatians 6:7

"Be not deceived; God is not mocked: for whatsoever a man soweth, that shall he also reap."

Chapter Six

1 John 3:18–19

"My little children, let us not love in word, neither in tongue; but in deed and in truth. [19]And hereby we know that we are of the truth, and shall assure our hearts before him."

2 Corinthians 9:6

"*But this I say, He which soweth sparingly shall reap also sparingly; and he which soweth bountifully shall reap also bountifully.*"

Galatians 6:7–9

"*Be not deceived; God is not mocked: for whatsoever a man soweth, that shall he also reap. 8For he that soweth to his flesh shall of the flesh reap corruption; but he that soweth to the Spirit shall of the Spirit reap life everlasting. 9And let us not be weary in well doing: for in due season we shall reap, if we faint not.*"

Matthew 12:33–37

"*Either make the tree good, and his fruit good; or else make the tree corrupt, and his fruit corrupt: for the tree is known by his fruit. 34O generation of vipers, how can ye, being evil, speak good things? for out of the abundance of the heart the mouth speaketh. 35A good man out of the good treasure of the heart bringeth forth good things: and an evil man out of the evil treasure bringeth forth evil things. 36But I say unto you, That every idle word that men shall speak, they shall give account thereof in the day of judgment. 37For by thy words thou shalt be justified, and by thy words thou shalt be condemned.*"

Ephesians Chapter 5

Be ye therefore followers of God, as dear children; 2And walk in love, as Christ also hath loved us, and hath given himself for us an offering and a sacrifice to God for a sweet-smelling savour.

3But fornication, and all uncleanness, or covetousness, let it not be once named among you, as becometh saints; 4Neither filthiness, nor foolish talking, nor jesting, which are not convenient: but rather giving of thanks. ⁵For this ye know, that no whoremonger, nor unclean person, nor covetous man, who is an idolater, hath any inheritance in the kingdom of Christ and of God. ⁶Let no man deceive you with vain words: for because of these things cometh the wrath of God upon the children of disobedience. ⁷Be not ye therefore partakers with them. ⁸For ye were sometimes darkness, but now are ye light in the Lord: walk as children of light: ⁹(For the fruit of the Spirit is in all goodness and righteousness and truth;) ¹⁰Proving what is acceptable unto the Lord. ¹¹And have no fellowship with the unfruitful works of darkness, but rather reprove them. ¹²For it is a shame even to speak of those things which are done of them in secret. ¹³But all things that are reproved are made manifest by the light: for whatsoever doth make manifest is light. ¹⁴Wherefore he saith, Awake thou that sleepest, and arise from the dead, and Christ shall give thee light.

¹⁵See then that ye walk circumspectly, not as fools, but as wise, ¹⁶Redeeming the time, because the days are evil. ¹⁷Wherefore be ye not unwise, but understanding what the will of the Lord is. ¹⁸And be not drunk with wine, wherein is excess; but be filled with the Spirit; ¹⁹Speaking to yourselves in psalms and hymns and spiritual songs, singing and making melody in your heart to the Lord; ²⁰Giving thanks always for all things unto God and the Father in the name of our Lord Jesus Christ; ²¹Submitting yourselves one to another in the fear of God.

²²Wives, submit yourselves unto your own husbands, as unto the Lord. ²³For the husband is the head of the wife, even as Christ is the head of the church: and he is the

saviour of the body. ²⁴*Therefore as the church is subject unto Christ, so let the wives be to their own husbands in every thing.*

²⁵*Husbands, love your wives, even as Christ also loved the church, and gave himself for it;* ²⁶*That he might sanctify and cleanse it with the washing of water by the word,* ²⁷*That he might present it to himself a glorious church, not having spot, or wrinkle, or any such thing; but that it should be holy and without blemish.* ²⁸*So ought men to love their wives as their own bodies. He that loveth his wife loveth himself.* ²⁹*For no man ever yet hated his own flesh; but nourisheth and cherisheth it, even as the Lord the church:* ³⁰*For we are members of his body, of his flesh, and of his bones.* ³¹*For this cause shall a man leave his father and mother, and shall be joined unto his wife, and they two shall be one flesh.* ³²*This is a great mystery: but I speak concerning Christ and the church.* ³³*Nevertheless let every one of you in particular so love his wife even as himself; and the wife see that she reverence her husband.*

CHAPTER SEVEN

1 PETER 3:7–12

"Likewise, ye husbands, dwell with them according to knowledge, giving honour unto the wife, as unto the weaker vessel, and as being heirs together of the grace of life; that your prayers be not hindered. ⁸*Finally, be ye all of one mind, having compassion one of another, love as brethren, be pitiful, be courteous:* ⁹*not rendering evil for evil, or railing for railing: but contrariwise blessing; knowing that ye are thereunto called, that ye should inherit a blessing.* ¹⁰*For he that will love life, and see good days, let him refrain his tongue from evil, and his lips that they speak no guile:* ¹¹*let him eschew evil, and do good; let him*

seek peace, and ensue it. [12]For the eyes of the Lord are over the righteous, and his ears are open unto their prayers: but the face of the Lord is against them that do evil."

MATTHEW 18:19

"Again I say unto you, That if two of you shall agree on earth as touching any thing that they shall ask, it shall be done for them of my Father which is in heaven."

PROVERBS 18:22

"Whoso findeth a wife findeth a good thing, and obtaineth favour of the Lord."

Dr. Myles Munroe
Spiritual Papa & Encourager

ABOUT THE AUTHOR

Jennie Staten is a believer and loves to share the hope given to us by trusting in Jesus Christ. Jennie leads a women's bible study, serves on the first impressions team at her church, and is active in volunteer services around her community.

She has written one other book: *Mama Come Home* and God has given her the title for her third book.

Jennie shares the passion that Jesus has for all His creation; that none should perish, but that all should come to repentance.